Praise for
CRYSTAL GRIDS
HOW AND WHY THEY WORK

"Wow! Finally a complete book about crystal grids that I can use in my classes! There is so much I could say! This is such a great book, so thorough and complete! This book is not only informative and full of science based facts that show 'Why and How Crystal Grids Work' but also full of great pictures, examples and wit as well. This book is a MUST HAVE for anyone wanting to learn why crystals can do what they do! Yay!"

--M. Flora Peterson, *Teacher, Author, Spiritual Empowerment Coach, Creator of The Yay Factor*™

"If you would like to read a simple, straightforward book about how and why to make crystal grids, look no further! Hibiscus Moon understands the logic behind using these high frequency tools to create a grid. This is a short-and-sweet little book on a topic that could be useful to just about anybody, because who wouldn't like to create a good feeling in their home, or a peaceful or healing place, or to attract greater prosperity?"

--Joy Gardner, author of *Vibrational Healing through the Chakras with Light, Color, Sound, Crystals and Aromatherapy*

D1301885

ISBN-13: 978-1463729189
ISBN-10: 1463729189

Hibiscus Moon © 2011-2012

DISCLAIMER:
The information in this book does not constitute medical advice, nor is it intended to take the place of medical or psychological treatment or act as replacement of legal or other expert advice. Every effort and attempt to ensure this book includes accurate information has been made, however mistakes and/or inaccuracies may well exist. The author accepts no liability or responsibility for any loss or damage caused or thought to be caused by the advice given in this book. It is recommended that any advice given be used in conjunction with expert advice.

www.HibiscusMoonCrystals.com

HIBISCUS MOON

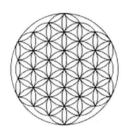

CRYSTAL GRIDS

HOW AND WHY THEY WORK: A SCIENCE-BASED, YET PRACTICAL GUIDE

CRYSTAL GRIDS
HOW AND WHY THEY WORK

For Frank, the love of my life, whom I've known since before I was even born; I love you more than the whole Multiverse!

FOREWORD

When I was asked to write a foreword to this edition I had no hesitation in agreeing. In every field there are gaps in understanding. They are the joys that drive us to further understand ourselves and the universe that surrounds us.

In *Crystal Grids, How and Why They Work*, Hibiscus Moon has delved into one of these gaps in the field of crystal healing and climbed out of a chasm of confusion to educate, illuminate and bring clarity to crystal grids.

Whether you are new to crystals or an experienced practitioner you'll find something new here to inform and stimulate.

Perhaps it's the way Hibiscus appraises the science behind crystal grids and keeps it approachable to the enthusiast as well as the expert reader.

Or maybe it's her Step by Step Guide and Practical Grid Recipes that are so clear and a joy to follow.

This is the sort of book that gives you an idea, creates a thought or possibility and points you on the path so you can travel the same road to whichever destination you are destined to reach.

Whether you need abundance or romance, or want to bring healing to people, animals and Mother Earth within the following pages you will find ideas to stimulate and methods to follow.

Love and crystal light,

Philip Permutt
Author of *The Crystal Healer: Crystal Prescriptions That Will Change Your Life Forever* and *Sacred Stones and Crystals*

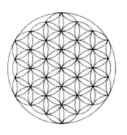

PART 1

THE "WHAT" OF CRYSTAL GRIDS

INTRODUCTION

I've been interested in crystals and stones from as far back as I can remember. Leafing through a Smithsonian Museum book of my father's at about the age of three, the amazing photographs of crystals and gems just stopped me in my tracks, riveting me to those pages! I would leaf through them over and over again, just staring until the pages were worn. They were much better than any children's book you could have ever plopped in front of me. Yes, I was kind of a strange child. Of course, I had no idea at the time what these beautiful objects were, but I later learned that they were created miraculously through Mother Earth's handiwork. I was intrigued that something as gorgeous and perfect as a crystal could emerge from the dirt and rough rocks.

I came back to crystals and stones later on with some undergraduate and graduate studies in geology. In becoming a science teacher, I even got to teach about them. Through teaching, I succeeded in getting my students just as excited about rocks and crystals as I was! *Well…not all of them.* A few of them still looked at me like I was a nerd, complete with glasses, pocket protector and lab coat holding my rocks…that's because I *was* one.

Ahem, still am.

I've always been very spiritual and have enjoyed exploring various fields of spirituality. In doing so, I noticed that crystals kept coming up again and again. Given my natural attraction to these gorgeous minerals born of nature's kitchen, I was captivated, so the lure of using them in spiritual practice was just too much. Of course I wanted to do that! However, I noticed that when crystals and stones were mentioned in metaphysical books or circles, the reasons given for why and how they worked seldom satisfied my curiosity and quest for knowledge.

I began blogging and vlogging about crystals just to connect with others who had the same interests as I did. Once I started down that path, whole new worlds started opening up to me; book recommendations, healing methods and new uses for working with crystals and stones. I had found a sort of blissful crystal treasure chest to rummage through! In starting my practice, I noticed that some things resonated with me immediately and others just didn't ring true. I experimented with various ways of working with the crystals and began realizing that the authors, books and methods that aligned with me most were the ones that seemed to be supported by physics and had scientific empirical explanations for why and how things worked. *Not surprising.* As I'm sure you've gathered by now, I prefer to take a scientific approach to working with crystals, researching and experimenting with how crystals work while also incorporating the metaphysical aspects. If "Physics" and "Metaphysics" had a gorgeous, brilliant, crystalline baby, that would describe my viewpoint beautifully!

One method of working with crystals that immediately interested me was that of crystal grids. Although the idea was mentioned a bit here and there, I could not find enough information to satiate my appetite for this knowledge and I just knew there was a strong correlation to science patiently waiting to be unearthed here, like a gorgeously sparkling giant quartz point. I did much experimenting on my own and found a few random videos on YouTube as well as some sporadic references in books, but this was not nearly enough. I took what information I was able to piece together and set off exploring various aspects and then experimenting on my own. This book is the result of that adventure.

What is a Crystal Grid?

From my work with crystal grids I devised a definition of what they are and how to best work with them:

A crystal grid is a geometric pattern of energetically aligned stones charged by intention set in a sacred space for the purpose of manifesting a particular objective.

I have thought long and hard about that definition and feel that it incorporates all of the elements that will allow a crystal grid to achieve optimal results.

So what's all this talk about "crystal grids"? Are we talking "magic" as in Harry-Potter-crystal-magic here? I often tell my students that "magic" is the word many like to give to unknown science. After all, an iPad would have been considered "magic" just one hundred years ago. Right? In fact, science fiction author Arthur C. Clarke declared, "Any sufficiently advanced technology is indistinguishable from magic".

A crystal grid incorporates the use of crystals and stones because of their precise vibratory frequency. Each stone has its own specific energy vibration which we can use for manifesting our intentions. The great thing about crystal grids is that you can use them to manifest almost any intention. In looking at my husband's utility knife and all its many uses, I realized that a crystal grid can be called the Swiss Army Knife of manifesting.

One of the first examples of a crystal grid that I read about was the World Peace Crystal Grid, founded by The International Center for Reiki Training (ICRT). This grid is a means by which Reiki practitioners and others can promote peace on Mother Earth via a crystal grid. Two grids were created and designated "Peace Grids". They were designed to allow Reiki to be transmitted to them and then stored. These grids were then positioned at the magnetic North and South Poles as well as in old Jerusalem for the specific purpose of promoting peace around the globe.

Their positions at the poles were chosen to make use of the earth's natural and potent electromagnetic field (EMF). Some view Mother Earth's EMF as her aura, or subtle energy. The poles of any magnet (including our earth magnet) are the most energetically powerful areas for magnetic force, thereby transporting the grid energy around the planet and restoring Mother Earth's EMF. (See Fig. 1). According to the ICRT, "the reservoir of healing energy it holds is available to empower all those working toward world healing and peace." *(http://www.reiki.org/globalhealing/northand southpolehomepage.html,* June 16, 2011)

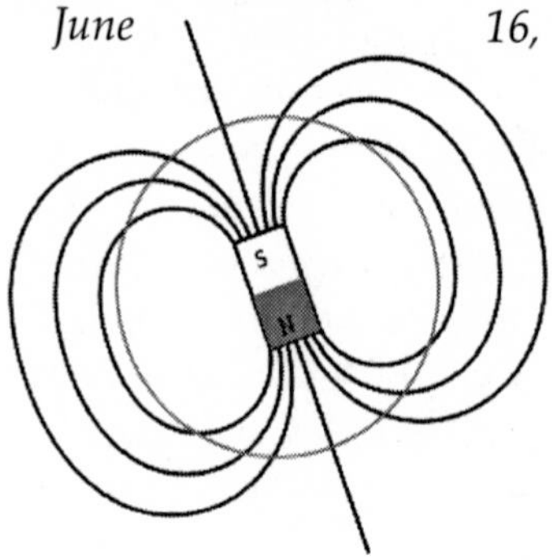

Fig. 1. Obtained from public domain, Wikimedia Commons, 2011

The Peace grids are 12" pure copper discs plated in 24-carat gold. (See Fig. 2). The discs are in the shape of the Hindu symbol for the heart chakra (a twelve-petaled lotus flower) with a crystal quartz pyramid in the center of each. The two quartz pyramids are cut from the same piece of rough quartz, thereby allowing them to be energetically aligned. Each of the twelve petals on the discs has a double-terminated quartz crystal attached. Then, under each of the quartz pyramids lies an inscription of the Usui Reiki power symbol as well as the Karuna Reiki peace symbol. Carved around the center are symbols for many different world religions along with this sentence: "May the followers of all religions and spiritual paths work together to create peace among all people on earth".

Fig. 2. Photo used with permission of William Lee Rand,
International Center for Reiki Training
http://www.reiki.org/GlobalHealing/Northandsouthpolehomepag
e.html

ICRT placed the grid at the North Pole in 1997, at the South Pole in 1999 and in Jerusalem in 2004. The idea is to give attention and focus to the grids and to send Reiki energy, if you are so inclined. In doing this, the grids are activated and keep peaceful energy flowing, like a circuit, to the entire planet. Please see the "Resources" section at the end of this book to read more about the World Peace Project and the ICRT.

CROP GRIDS

Although they don't involve crystals per se, crop formations or grids, also commonly known as "crop circles" (even though they're not always in circles) may also be "geometric patterns of energetically aligned formations charged by intention set in sacred space," and may have a connection to crystal grids in *how* they work.

Crop grids are large geometric patterns appearing inexplicably by means of flattening various types of crops (corn, rye, wheat, etc.). These formations started showing up around the 1970s, continue to occur to this day, and are considered to be a very interesting, yet difficult to explain phenomenon. The formations are usually created under the concealing cloak of night's darkness, so very few people actually claim to have seem them being made. According to Wikipedia, twenty-six countries have reported upwards of ten thousand crop formations since the phenomenon began (Wikipedia, 2011). For reasons unknown, numerous formations have appeared within close proximity to several sacred sites such as Avebury and Stonehenge. These sites are often reported to be energy vortices of sorts (more about that later in the section on "Sacred Geometry"). Could it be that the crop circles are attracted to these energy vortices or vice versa? Various hoaxers have been caught creating quite primitive crop formations by using a wooden board or crop roller to flatten the crops, but these never manage the complexity of formation that most crop circles adhere to. (See Fig. 3). In addition, no one has been able to fully explain this marvel. Many say that these complicated designs carry messages for us from beyond and that we should be paying more attention to them. The geometric patterns certainly do seem to be commonplace within our universe and appear to be the preferred method of communication among the energies; one might say they are the "Language of the Universe".

Fig. 3. Obtained from public domain, Wikimedia Commons, 2011

ENERGY FIELD OF A GRID

Whether we are speaking about crop grids, World Peace Grids or traditional crystal grids (ha! "traditional"), some scientists have noted that a three dimensional energy radius exists around all objects or beings (See Fig. 4). This energy field can be described as a torus, or a virtual "doughnut" of energy surrounding the object. This energy field corresponds to the object's or being's EMF (aka "aura"). The field size is dependant upon - the size, specific molecular make-up, and dominant oscillary rate (or base resonanant frequency) of the object or entity. So in this case, SIZE DOES MATTER! Therefore, the larger the crystal or stone, the larger the energy field around it. To get technical for just a second, a torus is a three-dimensional rotating shell of sorts, created by energy gyrating around a central axis. This "central axis" aspect is why I feel it is very important to have a center stone in our crystal grids, but we'll get to that later in the section on "Grid Components". In that section, we'll also cover a method you can use to exponentially amplify the energy field around your grid if you feel that the energy torus around the stones you are using may be too small or weak.

There are plenty of ways to measure energy. To specifically measure energy around a crystal grid, I have found that it's easiest to employ the help of some inexpensive copper dowsing rods. Dowsing rods have been used for thousands of years to locate various resources such as ground water, minerals, buried treasures and many other materials. Dowsing rods have also been used to pick up on naturally gridded energy currents of radiation emanating from Mother Earth, sometimes also referred to as ley lines.

Fig. 4. Image author, Fropuff, made available on Wikimedia Commons 2011

Modern dowsing rods are usually L-shaped. Copper dowsing L-rods are my preference due to copper's excellent energy conductivity compared to its relatively low cost. There are better energy conductors, for instance gold or silver, but their expense makes their use prohibitive. Please check the "Resources" section at the end of this book to find out where to get a good pair of copper dowsing rods.

To measure the energy around a crystal grid using your dowsing rods, stand about 25 feet away from the crystal grid, or more if it is a particularly large grid. Hold the short ends of the "L" loosely in your hands and leave the long ends to rotate freely, so that they can be influenced by the energy in their immediate environment. Hold the rods' long ends steady and parallel with the ground while pointing them at the grid. Be sure that you are completely relaxed, taking several deep breaths to get yourself into the proper state of being. Once the rods stop quivering and the energy relaxes, begin walking slowly towards your grid and make note of any movement in the dowsing rods. Once you notice this movement, move back a bit and then slowly move forward again. Does the rod movement occur again at the same distance from your grid? If so, you've most likely just discovered the energy torus' edge (think of it as an invisible force field.) Therefore, by measuring the energy torus around a particular crystal grid you can determine if certain crystals and/or geometric patterns generate more or less energy for you. This makes a handy tool to have when experimenting with various grids. Please see the "Resources" section for my video on how I use dowsing rods to sense energy around a crystal grid.

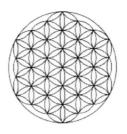

PART 2

THE "WHY" OF CRYSTAL GRIDS

SACRED GEOMETRY

Sacred geometry refers to geometric structures holding a cosmic significance. Many ancient as well as modern cultures adhere to sacred geometric forms in their architecture as well as in other endeavors. In fact, it's often observed as the very building blocks of nature. Geometric patterns appear to be commonplace within our universe, seeming to be the favored means of energy transmission. Sacred geometry may actually be nature's means of manifesting a universal plan, tapping into just the right frequency necessary to communicate with source energy. Once again, sacred geometry seems to be the universe's language. This is why I feel it is so important to use sacred geometry when constructing our crystal grids. It allows for clear communication.

Here are some remarkable examples of sacred geometry "doing its thing". Allegedly, the creation of the first eight cells of an embryo, known as the blastocyst or morula, is approximately the point at which the embryo begins to radiate electrical impulses (See Fig. 5). There have been scientific studies which show that although electrical resistance is present from the first cell division, there is a spike of resistance precisely at the 8-cell stage and then rises progressively from there (Hori, Ito, 1966). To many, these electrical impulses represent the point at which the soul's energy enters the physical plane. This actually corresponds with many ancient cultural and religious teachings. What is extremely noteworthy is that the morula, (stages "c - e" in Fig. 5) looks very similar to a symbol commonly known as the "Flower of Life" aka the Star of David, Star Tetrahedron or Merkaba (see Figs 6 and 7). Due to this similarity, the inner circles of this symbol are often referred to as "The Seed of Life". The oldest known depictions of this symbol can be found on the walls of the temple of the Osirion at Abydos in Egypt. It is also notable that the original morula cell cluster actually remains within a point at the base of the spine throughout development, relating to the location of our Root Chakra. The connection between the morula and the Root Chakra is interesting to note because our Root Chakra purportedly governs the first seven years of our life, our developmental stage, forming the foundation for our feelings towards basic survival and essential needs, which is *exactly* what the Root Chakra energies relate to. All these associations cause me to contemplate that there is some sort of deep underlying meaning and/or exchange of vital information here.

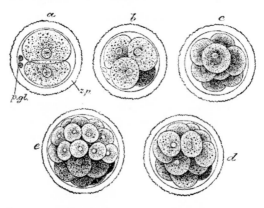

Fig. 5. First stages of division of mammalian embryo. Faithful reproduction of a lithograph plate from Gray's Anatomy. Obtained from public domain, Wikimedia Commons, 2011

Fig. 6. Flower of Life. Obtained from public domain,
Wikimedia Commons, 2011

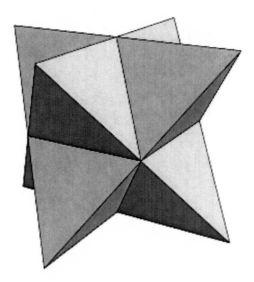

Fig. 7. Merkaba. Image author, Fropuff, made available on
Wikimedia Commons 2011

Italian Renaissance "Do-It-All-Genius", Leonardo da Vinci, took his cue from the ancients and seemed to also be very intrigued by the Flower of Life, spending much time studying and captivated by its form, elegance and mathematics. (See Fig. 8). Using this symbol in his drawings he realized that geometric forms could be derived from the Flower of Life symbol. These forms happened to be the five Platonic Solids, along with the sphere, the all-important torus as well as the Golden Ratio of Phi, which he used extensively in his drawings and architecture.

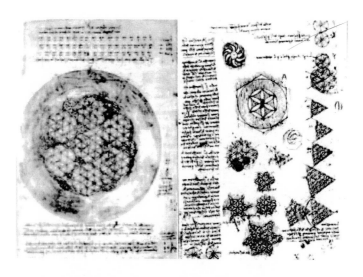

Fig. 8. Leonardo da Vinci's drawing and thoughts on the Flower of Life. Obtained from public domain, Wikimedia Commons, 2011

We can also use sacred geometry to look at the human body as Da Vinci did in much of his artwork, most notably in his famous drawing, "Vetruvian Man".

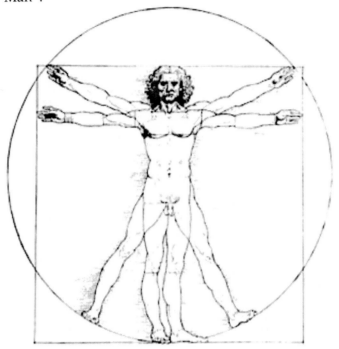

Fig. 9. Vitruvian Man by Leonardo da Vinci. Obtained from public domain, Wikimedia Commons, 2011

You will note that in the very center of the square in DaVinci's drawing (the root chakra area) is the point where the morula is said to reside. *In the very center.* Da Vinci's drawing of the human figure was founded on the relationship of the perfect human body proportions aligning with sacred geometric measurements, namely the Divine Proportion. As Da Vinci showed us so well, the human body seems to be designed following the principles of sacred geometry and a number ratio known as the Golden Ratio or Divine Proportion, wherein the relation of the longer side to the shorter side is this Golden Ratio, aka Phi (approximately 1.6180339887) and represented by this symbol: φ. For instance, Phi is the proportion of your hand to forearm or of each successive bone in your finger, to take just two from many other examples within the human body. Phi is expressed in everything from atoms, to the vast expanse of the universe. It is said that this ratio expresses "Universal Law" as well as beauty and wholeness in nature. We even see the ratio appear in the proportions of chemical compounds, geometry of crystals, harmonious chords of music and in the vibrational frequencies of light. What is known as the Fibonacci Sequence is a series of numbers related to the Golden Ratio. The numbers of this sequence are arrived at by taking the first two numbers and adding them together to get the next number: 0, 1, 1, 2, 3, 5, 8, 13, continuing indefinitely. The ratio between each number in the sequence comes closer and closer to 1.618 the higher you go in the sequence and there's its connection to the Golden Ratio. The Fibonacci Sequence reveals itself in nature repeatedly as in the lineages of bees. For instance, a female bee has two gendered parents (a male and a female), but a male bee has only a female parent. When we count up the number of parents and grandparents for each generation, you get a number from the Fibonacci Sequence every single time. We also see Fibonacci numbers appearing in the number of clockwise spirals on the head of a sunflower. If you count the counterclockwise spirals you'll get the neighboring Fibonacci number. Pretty wild, huh? Countless creators of architecture and art have made use of this ratio when designing their works, having noted its use in nature and finding it to be the most visually satisfying and aesthetically pleasing, therefore emulating it. There are numerous other instances found throughout the cosmos such as the spiral design of a Nautilus shell and the spiral proportions in some spiral galaxies just name a few. Check the "Resources" section at the end of this book to find out where you can see many more examples.

Astonishingly, the latest galaxy-cluster mapping of our universe has revealed sacred geometry in its cosmic blueprint! As I noted before, this design seems to be a universal preference as recent microwave data collected via satellite has suggested. This new information is indicating that our known universe is in the shape of an enormous dodecahedron, a twelve symmetrically-sided shape. All the while, the "voids" between galaxies suggest jam-packed, side by side octahedrons, eight symmetrically-sided shapes. (See Fig. 10, 11 and 12.) This type of design structure is known as "Space Frame truss-work", pun intended (space, outer space, get it?). This type of construction is recognized as being extremely sturdy yet very lightweight, possibly the most efficient architectural design ever. No wonder our universe configured itself in this way. These shapes all belong to that group called the Platonic Solids (tetrahedron, cube, octahedron, icosahedron, dodecahedron) so revered by Plato himself (c. 427 BC – c. 347 BC, more about him in the section on "Mother Earth's Grid"). In fact, Plato wrote in his dialogue Timaeus, that the dodecahedron was the most sacred form and is the very shape of our universe. This is amazing, isn't it? Please see the "Resources" section at the end of this book to read more about this particular marvel. Reference:

(http://www.miqel.com/space_photos_maps/gal actic_info/position-of-milky-way-in-virgo-supercluster.html 2011)

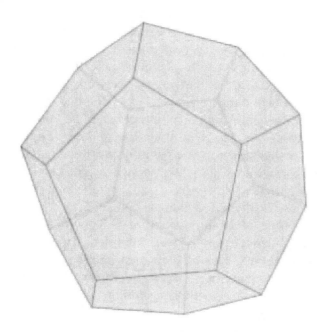

Fig. 10. Dodecahedron, a polyhedron with twelve identical equilateral pentagon faces, Obtained from public domain, Wikimedia Commons, 2011.

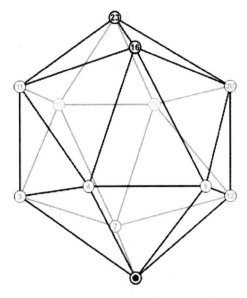

Fig. 11. Icosahedron, a polyhedron with twenty identical equilateral triangle faces. Obtained from public domain, Wikimedia Commons, 2011. Author, Lipedia

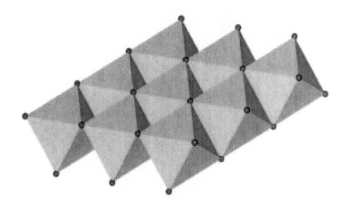

Fig. 12. Closely packed octahedrons, Obtained from public domain, Wikimedia Commons, 2011. Author, Lipedia.

It appears as though sacred geometry has set the stage for an extremely coherent energy field. In addition, remember that crystals are naturally-occurring inorganic solids whose atoms are also arranged in an orderly, geometric, repeating pattern; the Platonic Solids themselves. *Do we detect a theme here?* Sacred geometry is part of their structure. Of course it is! I feel this geometric structure is what allows crystals to communicate so easily within a grid configuration and, in turn, to communicate with the entire universe and, ultimately, with source energy.

"Crystalline forms are the key patterns for the way the energies are built in the universe; and the key to unlocking energy in a constructive way."
-- Dr. William A. Tiller, Professor Emeritus of Materials Science and Engineering at Stanford University.

MOTHER EARTH'S GRID

According to ancient teachings and to more recent metaphysical researchers, Mother Earth is surrounded by a web of energetic grid lines intersecting at specific points creating a type of power matrix. Some say this matrix may be originating from Mother Earth's own crystalline iron core, radiating light-information that some beings can actually tune into if they are well grounded. The first known mention of this matrix/grid was made by our friend, Plato, who contemplated its existence after discovering information he claimed came from the lost Atlantis. According to some Plato interpretations, the Atlanteans had completely gridded Mother Earth using specific grid intersections to select locations for various "power sites" such as pyramids and other sacred sites. This earth grid is also mentioned by other ancient cultures such as the Hopi Indians, the Chinese, Australian aborigines, the Mayans and the Egyptians.

The earth grid has resurfaced again and again over the years. In the 1980's it was re-examined extensively by the husband and wife team of Professors Bethe Hagens and William S. Becker. Basing their work on previous explorations done in the 1970's by Russian researchers, Hagens and Becker continued investigating the use of sacred geometry to construct the ultimate-earth grid. This grid interconnected two geometric patterns, an icosahedron with a dodecahedron (yes, there they are again!) Adding yet another sacred geometric shape, the polyhedron, results in a grid with sixty-two intersections from which to work with. This design is known as the "Unified Vector Geometry 120 Polyhedron", aka the 'Earth Star'. (See Fig. 13). The intersections and grid lines, aka ley lines, are comparable to the meridians of energy and points used in Chinese acupuncture for the human body. These earth intersection points and grid lines appear to correspond with many well known "power sites" or energy vortices on the planet. Here is just a sampling of some of these sites:

❖ Great Pyramid at Giza
❖ Lake Baikal, the planet's deepest, largest and oldest (30 million years old!) lake in Southern Siberia, Russia
❖ Several points outlining the Mid-Atlantic Ocean Ridge
❖ The Bermuda Triangle of the Atlantic Ocean
❖ Hawaii's time-warp zone
❖ Wilpena Pound; an impact crater in South Australia
❖ Easter Island megaliths.

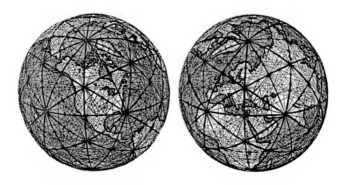

Fig. 13. The Earth Star. Image used with permission of Bethe Hagens and William S. Becker.

According to many metaphysicists, this earth grid is important to humanity because, acting as a crystalline matrix of information, it has the ability to reflect and magnify our consciousness. In fact, Mother Earth's grid perfectly demonstrates how to set up a crystal grid. It makes use of a center stone with its iron crystalline core along with a geometric pattern of energetically aligned energy vortices to communicate with our consciousness and transmitting information to source energy. That's one BIG crystal grid!

TAPPING INTO SOURCE ENERGY

Crystal grids permit us to easily tap into source energy, allowing us to communicate with energy across space and time. Many of us know this is possible but are not sure of *how*. A theory regarding a subtle energy field, known as the morphic field, can help explain the "how and why" of it.

Biochemist Rupert Sheldrake proposes that, as energetic beings, we're all connected to each other and energy via this morphic field. Without getting too detailed *and boring you to death with biogenetics*, Sheldrake's theory is based on a process known as 'morphogenesis', which is the concept that embryonic cells of any particular organism have a prearranged spatial distribution, sort of a prearranged energetic blueprint for the cells to follow as the organism grows, acting as a kind of template for a particular organism. Sheldrake suggests that the morphic field exists within and around all energetic forms and is responsible for the coordination of physical and behavioral traits.

He also maintains that this field is created by the recurrence of repeated, similar actions or thoughts. Sheldrake further proposes that a specific energetic unit will automatically locate and instinctively "harmonize" with its corresponding morphic field. Therefore, our own energetic bodies are constantly adapting, adjusting, altering and being affected by our own human morphic field. This all helps to explain where organisms get the natural instincts they're born with such as birds and sea turtles knowing exactly where to migrate to and when.

Could they be tapping into this morphic field? Tapping into source energy?

This is where the popular yet speculative idea of the "Hundredth Monkey Effect" ties in. To quickly explain, Japanese researchers noticed that when one individual within a group of wild monkeys learned how to do something, s/he passed that knowledge onto other monkeys within the group. However, by the time one hundred monkeys had learned this new behavior, monkeys throughout the entire population, even on other islands, would instinctively know how to model the same behavior *without being taught by others*. The scientific observation techniques used to monitor the Hundredth Monkey Effect are considered questionable by some due to non-empirical observation techniques, but it's an intriguing idea which has some merit and which meshes nicely with this whole morphic field theory.

The concept of morphogenesis and a morphic field accounts for *the communication system* used in distance healing as well as other psychic phenomenon and is something we can tap into when using our crystal grids. In addition, these concepts support the belief of a universal power, God, source energy, collective consciousness, "The Force" (had to sneak a Star Wars reference in here!) and many other possible names and concepts; I feel the labeling is all semantics anyway. Tapping into this morphic field may be the "telephone line" that source energy uses to allow our crystal grids to get their messages across. Physicist David Bohm proposes the theory of a "Holographic Universe", whereby information can be recorded and later reconstructed when the original information field is no longer present. He suggests that this holographic information may be embedded in the very fabric of space/time. Perhaps the morphic field is how this holographic information gets communicated.

"What happens in just a small fragment of the holographic energy interference pattern affects the entire structure simultaneously; there is a tremendous connectivity relationship between all parts of the holographic universe."
--Author Richard Gerber, *Vibrational Medicine*

Can you see the possibilities here in working with your crystal grid? Accessing the field, or the holographic nature of the cosmos, allows us to not be concerned with space and time and possibly access different dimensions! The ability of some people to engage in remote viewing; that is the ability to "view" information or a specific scene regarding a distant target using extrasensory perception; is further evidence of the morphic field and the holographic nature of our cosmic existence. By using a crystal grid, we can purposefully access this field, communicate with it effectively and direct energy appropriately, positively affecting a person or situation wherever it may be across space and time.

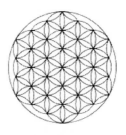

PART 3

THE "HOW" OF CRYSTAL GRIDS

INTENTION SETTING

One of the first steps you must take before constructing your crystal grid is to firmly decide what your precise intention is. What do you want to bring about? A crystal grid can be used for just about any purpose you can dream up. You must be very unambiguous and have a specific goal in mind in order to communicate it to source energy. Make sure your intention is super-clear and unmistakable. If your intention is wavering or muddied then you can be sure that the "smoke signals" will get crossed and the result will be lack-luster. Here is a short list of some possible intentions, but the sky's the limit:

- ❖ Prosperity & Abundance
- ❖ Health & Vitality
- ❖ Compassion & Love for Others
- ❖ Romance
- ❖ Self Love
- ❖ Mental Clarity
- ❖ Purification & Protection
- ❖ Confidence Boost
- ❖ New Career
- ❖ Climb Career Ladder
- ❖ Chakra Balancing
- ❖ Mother Earth/World Healing
- ❖ Relationships with Angels or Spirits
- ❖ Spiritual Growth

Now let me throw in here that when using a grid, or any other means to try to manifest a certain outcome, be certain you are not intentionally setting out to interfere with anyone else's free will.

For example, if you choose to create a grid to make yourself more open to receiving love into your life, that's perfectly fine, but do not set about creating a grid to make someone else love you. That is interfering with someone else's free will. Many cultures and religions teach that attempting such a thing brings about bad karma. Who wants to mess around with bad karma? Trying to influence another's choices will cause more challenges in the long run than you attempted to solve in the first place. So the whole thing backfires. Worry about yourself and only yourself; never attempt to control anyone else for any reason. Many of us have had to learn this the hard way; you can only control yourself, so only set up crystal grids that control *you* and *your* situation.

As author Jack Canfield tells us so wisely, you really only have power over three simple things in your life – the thoughts you think, the imagery you imagine, and the actions you take. That's it. Conveniently, we make use of all three of those things when working with our crystal grids. So we're going to keep our noses clean and stay within those parameters.

One possible intention for your crystal grid may be to send distance healing. This type of healing is non-invasive and will not interfere with any other healing modalities, actually complimenting and working alongside traditional and other alternative health practices. Unlike drugs and some medical practices, contra-indication is not a concern when working with crystal grid energies. As I explained earlier, a healing crystal grid will allow us to tap into that source energy, sending our good intentions across space and time.

In addition, when you are doing a crystal grid for the good of someone other than yourself, let's say for healing; always get the permission of the individual. You don't know what that person's intentions are and they should be aligned with yours. This is so the goal can be clearly communicated to source energy; if this weren't the case, it may bring about unexpected and possibly very messy outcomes. The only time that I would overlook this is if we were attempting to bring about peace or healing for a very large group or for the entire planet.

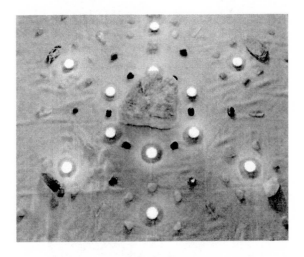

The center of a very large half-room sized Love grid I created for a group love-focused meditation using a pink cloth with a very large rose quartz as the center stone surrounded by more rose quartz (some heart-shaped), rhodonite, clear quartz, jade & green aventurine using the hexagon pattern.

Here we see the very same large rose quartz specimen, whom I've dubbed Big Mama, who weighs 18.5lbs being used in various other simpler love grids.

GRID FORMATIONS

There are as many ways to set up your crystal grid as there are types of minerals (hovering around 4000). Actually, the sheer quantity of minerals gives us an almost infinitesimal number of possible ways to set up your crystal grid. For all the reasons stated previously, I prefer to use a sacred geometric pattern as my template. There are also many other shapes and designs you can use. I've listed my favorites here. Please also check the "References" in the back of this book for a link to download some free printable templates I provide. A quick online search will also turn up many more that you may feel will be more suitable to your specific intention.

Hexagonal grids. A hexagon is a six-sided geometric shape. I prefer to use quartz in conjunction with a hexagonal pattern due to quartz's crystal system also being hexagonal. I feel this sets up extremely clear communication for all the energies present within the grid. Why make it a Tower of Babel affair? We want to get your message across with the least amount of resistance thereby making the manifesting that much quicker. Makes sense, right?

A hexagonal pattern can be used for any intention. Interestingly, in the 1980s the Voyager missions detected an enormous hexagonal pattern of clouds on Saturn's North Pole, larger than Mother Earth! (See Fig. 14). Scientists have recently been able to recreate similar polygon shapes in a lab setting using "fluid dynamics", and allege that these hexagons can even appear in hurricanes. Yet, why are they not appearing in fluids everywhere all the time?

Scientists aren't yet able to explain the reason for this anomaly.

However, these aren't just any old Saturnian clouds. These clouds don't shift in latitude like Saturn's other clouds do. Rather, they stay put while rotating at the same frequency as Saturn's radio emissions. Does this mean the hexagon is transmitting information? Does it have a higher purpose? Why a hexagon? Just asking.

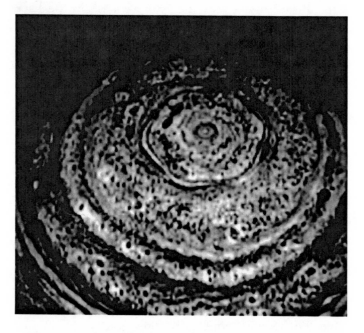

Fig. 14. Photo credited to NASA. Obtained from public domain, Wikimedia Commons, 2011

With a hexagonal template, you may place one stone in the center (the center stone) and six at each point around the perimeter of the shape. (See Fig. 15). With any crystal grid design, you may simply create the shape on a computer and print it out or draw it by hand using a ruler and possibly a drafting compass (if you're drawing circles) to use as a template for placing your crystals on. I do feel that drawing your own design template adds yet another layer of your intentional energy, making your grid that much stronger.

You can leave your template under your grid all the time or carefully slide it out after you've placed your crystals. It's up to you. Some people prefer to have nothing beneath their grid at all. So this is personal preference.

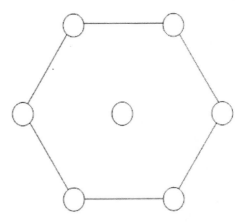

Fig. 15. Possible Crystal Placement for a Hexagon Template, the circles represent crystal placement.

Flower of Life. Another sacred geometric pattern you may be drawn to is the previously discussed Flower of Life. (See Fig. 16.) This design is created by overlapping evenly-spaced circles. From this patterning of circles emerges a symmetrical flower-like pattern looking similar to a hexagon. Again, this pattern may be used for any intention. Drawing your own Flower of Life will provide you with an extremely powerful template. You can simply place your center stone and then put the other stones around the design wherever you feel called to do so, while making sure to keep them symmetrical.

Fig. 16. Obtained from public domain, Wikimedia Commons, 2011

Five-Pointed Star or Square. I've paired these two shapes together because they are very complementary for attaining protection and purification of energies. The five-pointed star also has the added benefit, according to many cultures, of bringing about higher states of consciousness and deep meditation, which will be useful for transmuting any negative energies in your environment. It will thereby bring about a purified atmosphere.

If you are looking to add the dimension of stability to your environment, I suggest using a square grid because this has been used by ancient cultures as the symbol of strength, structure and permanence. Placing your stones in these patterns would be the same as with the hexagonal pattern: place a center stone and then one crystal or stone on each point along the perimeter.

Spirals. If you're looking for expansion, creativity or to add a feminine quality to your grid, a spiral pattern would be a good choice. Nikolai Kosyrev, a Russian astronomer/astrophysicist, noted that the spiral is another persistent yet distinct pattern in the universe. He regarded it as a "physical manifestation of time" and stated that the very fabric of "space-time" is a spiraled vortex. In addition, ancient cultures connect the spiral with positive feminine energy and with a Mother Earth connection.

When working with spiral energy, I don't use just any old spiral, but I go back to my Sacred Geometry Crayon Box and pull out the very precise Phi Spiral that makes use of the Golden Ratio we discussed earlier. Doing this allows us, once again, to use the lingo that the universe really seems to jive with. In doing so we are also possibly using the most-favored design of source energy to do our translating. Indeed, the Fibonacci Sequence or Golden Ratio (Phi Ratio of 1.618) we spoke of earlier can be expressed as a spiral. You may remember that the ratio between each number in the Fibonacci sequence comes closer and closer to 1.618 the higher you go in the sequence. You create the Phi Spiral design when using this ratio to create it. (See Fig. 17.) We often see this spiral in nature with the arrangement of branches on trees, the placement of stems of plants, DNA molecules, in pine cones and on and on. Yet again, since it appears so often, it would seem that the Phi ratio is easily understood and recognized throughout the universe. It may be that this ratio is specifically tuned to a precise frequency, allowing it to be broadcast across space and time in order to manifest whatever need be.

To place your stones on the spiral, simply begin with your center stone in the middle, or very beginning point of the spiral and radiate outward with the positioning of the other stones.

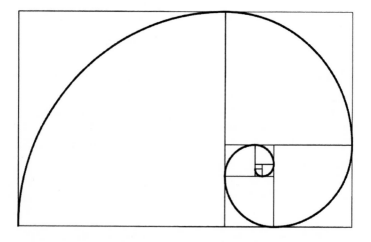

Fig. 17. Phi spiral, using Golden Ratio. Obtained from public domain, Wikimedia Commons, 2011

Leminscate (infinity symbol) or Circle. Each of these two shapes can be used to bring about endless abundance of anything at all, such as prosperity, love, health, wealth and many other intentions. For millennia, the circle has been the symbol of unity, perfection and the infinite. It also represents Mother Earth's cycles. Another symbol that represents the "never-ending" is the figure-eight-on-its-side infinity symbol also known as the Leminscate (see Fig. 18). In ancient India and Tibet, this symbol represented flawlessness along with the duality and unity between male and female. Therefore, either of these symbols makes an ideal crystal grid template perfect for bringing about prosperity and abundance in any area of your life. Again, the center stone would be placed directly on the intersection and then the other stones positioned along the perimeter of the design.

Fig. 18. Obtained from public domain, Wikimedia Commons, 2011

Above: A prosperity and abundance grid using citrine and green aventurine.

Below: an Intuitive Relationship grid using rose quartz and amethyst.

GRID COMPONENTS

In order to create a crystal grid you will need several items. Firstly, you will need your **center stone**. I feel that no matter what design template you choose to use, you should always have a center stone present. Remember that whole bit about the torus of energy around your crystal grid? That virtual "doughnut" of energy revolves around a central axis, which will now be your chosen center stone. This piece will be your all-important communicator acting as the broadcaster for your grid's intentions, sort of like a radio transmission tower. Those large radio-transmitting towers transform electric energy into a radio frequency that can be picked up by radio receivers. Your center stone will be performing essentially the same job, transforming your intentions into a vibrational frequency and broadcasting them into the universe, to source energy. For this reason, I feel it's important that your center stone be the most prominent piece in your grid, centrally located and larger than the other pieces. Use your intuition to determine how large, but remember, in this case, *size does matter*.

Secondly, you will need your **surrounding stones**. How many stones you will need is dependent on your personal preferences and the design you chose to use. If it appeals to you and you are called to do so, you can build upon your basic template, making your design more complex and intricate. You may choose to add more dimensions and expand on your design by adding another ring or layer of stones around the first. This is perfectly OK, as long as you adhere to the same original design template.

Some people choose to add another component to help powerfully reflect or magnify their intentions. This can be done by adding a **mirror** or even a **magnifying glass.** This could be placed under your entire crystal grid; alternatively, a small one could fit under just the center stone.

Next, you will need to decide upon the **location** of your grid. I always suggest putting your grid in what you deem to be your sacred space, whether that is a room you have designed specifically for that purpose or a tiny corner of your closet so that kids and pets don't tear the whole thing apart. Wherever it is, make it *sacred* to you. You may choose to light candles or incense there, meditate in this area, pray, play calming music; whatever represents "sacredness" to you.

Some also suggest aligning your grid with the north/south magnetic alignment of the planet. Why not? This makes a lot of sense to me since you are able to take advantage of the magnetic energies of Mother Earth to powerfully intensify your grid. All you need is an inexpensive **compass** to find Magnetic North. Now, please don't use one of those freebie pieces of junk found at the bottom of a Cracker Jack box (they're free for a reason). Use a good compass if you want reliable, relevant information. Once you've located Magnetic North, simply align your crystal grid and yourself in the same direction as the needle points on your compass. Do this whenever working with the grid.

NOTE: When working with a compass, be certain that, of course, you're not near any other magnets, speakers, large metal objects or electronics. Be careful not to wear any belt buckles, metal jewelry, or watches since all of these items can meddle with the magnetic field and may cause your compass to point to a false "North". Note, too, that Mother Earth's Magnetic North position fluctuates from time to time, so you'll need to keep watch and frequently recheck your placement. At the time of this writing, Mother Earth's magnetic North Pole shift has been ever-increasing in speed and is now shifting at up to more than 35 miles per year! So you will need to keep close tabs on that.

Next, you'll need an **activation wand**. This is the crystal or device you will use to direct your intentions and energy into your grid as well as "turn it on". A wand is actually an extension of your EMF intermingled with its own energy, allowing you to project intention into your grid. A crystal, mineral or stone wand is ideal because it will direct, move and amplify the energies of your grid. For ease of transmission and communication, an activation wand should ideally be the same type of crystal or stone that you are also using in your grid.

For example, if you are using rose quartz in your grid then your wand can also be made of rose quartz or have rose quartz incorporated within it. Your activation wand can be a natural crystal with a terminated end or one that is cut and polished as a wand for this very purpose. It is easy to find these in a local rock shop or with a simple search for "crystal wand" online. If the retail outlet you choose doesn't have the specific crystal or stone wand you're looking for, ask the owners if they can special order it for you. You may also find or make a wand out of wood, glass or copper and top it with a crystal.

You may also want to have two or three wands for varying purposes, depending on the intentions of your grids. For example, if you tend to often use clear quartz crystal and black tourmaline in your grids, you may want to have a wand made of each and then, perhaps a copper wand as more of a neutral piece for any other types of grids.

If you are creating a crystal grid for another person, for example to help heal someone or to send them abundant self-love, it will be very helpful to have a **photo** of that person looking happy and in good health. In fact, it's a good idea to be sure the photo was taken while the person was healthy. In a pinch you can also just simply have their name written on a slip of paper. If your grid is for sending energy to a particular location on the planet, for instance sending healing energy to the people hurt by an earthquake in a specific location, you can use a map of that area placed under your grid. If your grid's purpose is to generate peace and healing for the entire planet, then a photo of Mother Earth would be ideal. These photos and names should be placed under your center stone.

To further amplify your crystal grid and exponentially increase the energy torus around it, I suggest the use of an **outer crystal grid** that will surround your main inner grid and magnify its energies. This is certainly not necessary, but it is especially helpful if the stones you have available are very small or if you are concerned that their energy won't be powerful enough to do the job. I choose to make my outer grids of clear crystal quartz due to this mineral's ability to amplify energy.

The outer grid should follow the same design template that your main grid follows. So for example, if your main inner grid is a hexagon, then you will create your outer grid using six clear crystal quartz pieces in a larger hexagon pattern around your main grid, perhaps around the perimeter of the room with your main grid erected in the very center of the room. (See Fig. 19.) The outer grid can be just a bit larger than your main inner grid, or it can be as large as the room or space you're working in. This is entirely up to you. Beware, however, that if you do use an entire room or space for your grid, every time you enter that room, you will be entering the energy field of the grid. Sometimes, this sort of set up is not very practical; consequently, we work with what we have and where we have it, making up for it in other ways. Additionally, when activating your grid, don't overlook activating the outer grid as well. I'll discuss exactly how to do that in the section on "Activating and Maintaining Your Grid".

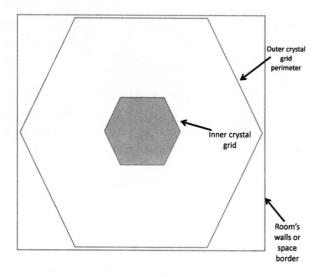

Fig. 19. Outer and main inner crystal grid layout.

How to Choose Crystals for Your Grid

At this point you may be wondering how to go about deciding exactly which crystals to use in your crystal grid. There are several ways to this. I feel the most powerful way to choose your crystals, and the way in which will probably yield the best results, is to choose your crystals *intuitively*. You may be able to "feel" or sense, which crystals belong; or you may get certain messages, "knowings" or visions of which stones to use. Do not ignore this gut instinct. Follow it. It's there, nagging at you, for a reason. Meditation may help you with intuiting which stones to use. During a meditative session, you may get an image or message that you may not have received otherwise, so try this method before you push intuition aside.

If you are simply not getting any intuitive messages about which stones to use then you can always research the written properties of crystals and stones in books. There is a plethora of crystal books and information online to choose from. You will notice that some of the information is contradictory, so try to use highly recommended books and resources and also look for a common thread among these sources. If it's mentioned in several different, well-respected books that rose quartz is good for bringing about love and compassion, then this is probably so for most of the population. It may not be so for *everyone* and that is why I feel intuition is a more reliable method.

Please check the "Resources" section at the end of this book for a list of some books that I highly recommend for this purpose.

Using a pendulum or dowsing rods can be very helpful in helping you to decide which crystals to include because these tools help you to connect to your higher self, tapping into answers you already know on a super-conscious level. You can spread out your possible crystal choices on a table (if you're using dowsing rods, you may need to place the crystals on separate tables and very far apart) and use your dowsing instrument to select the stones. If you're using a pendulum you can simply ask for a "Yes" or "No" answer as you hold your pendulum over each stone. If you choose to use the dowsing rods then you will be looking for energetic movement from them as you hold them above each stone. Movement will indicate that the stone would be beneficial to your grid. No activity from the rods would be a sign that you shouldn't include that stone. The more activity you get from the rods, the more that crystal should be included.

Using geological similarities among the crystals is another factor you can use to help you decide which crystals to use. For instance, I feel that minerals that belong to the same crystal system, species or of the same "crystal family" can energetically communicate with each other much more easily. I liken this to people who are from the same country who can all speak the same language and can get around easier because they know the lay of the land. They can correspond with each other more straightforwardly and work together more effectively than people who are from different countries because they can communicate easily. Similarly, crystals and stones will be able to communicate vibrational frequencies on a molecular level with more efficiency if they have geological similarities. Please see the "Resources" section for some good geological sources to determine crystal systems and "crystal families".

Here I created a more elaborate and large prosperity grid (4 feet across) in the middle of a room using green satin and a green Flower of Life grid as the template.
The crystals used were pyrite, green aventurine, citrine, jade and clear quartz.

For this grid, I chose to do a simple hexagon design to help heal the waters and organisms after the Gulf of Mexico Oil Gusher. This grid used clear quartz as the center stone surrounded by chrysocolla, lepidolite and smokey quartz.

You may view a video I did about this grid here:
http://youtu.be/VWpIG1f_1vk

Activating and Maintaining Your Grid

So you're in your prepared sacred space. You've got all your grid components with chosen crystals and stones. You've created a sacred space facing Magnetic North (if you've chosen to do that). You have chosen your activation wand and you will be using it to connect all the energy channels with intention in order to activate and energetically connect the crystals within your grid. You'll now want to go into a tranquil state by meditating or just relaxing for a few minutes. This will allow your brain to descend into alpha brainwaves, allowing you to achieve a state of focused attention and intuition.

In order to activate or trigger your grid, you will need an "affirmation", a short positive statement summarizing what it is you would like your crystal grid to bring about. Be sure your affirmation is stated in a positive way. For instance, rather than stating, "I will not belittle, hold myself back and second-guess myself any longer" you can say "Through self-support and abundant motivation I will manifest all my dreams!" With your activation wand in hand and while stating your well thought-out affirmation, point the activation wand at the center stone and visualize energy beaming from your body into the wand, out through its apex and into your center stone. Then move your wand from stone to stone as if you were playing "Connect-the-Dots", "linking up" energy from one stone to the next closest stone, preferably in a clockwise direction. Continue moving the wand, playing energetic-connect-the-dots until you have united all the stones within your grid, repeating your affirmation the whole time. An alternative way to do this is to say or read your affirmation with focused intent and then concentrate on activating your grid by energetically connecting the crystals.

While activating, you won't actually be touching the stones with the wand. You're simply directing the flow of energy into the grid and guiding it into the sacred geometric pattern you've set up, all the while stating your affirmation. As I mentioned, when you state your affirmation, be sure to do it with focused visualization and true intention infusing emotion into it as this will set the correct thought forms and vibrational frequencies necessary to trigger your grid. Please see the "Resources" section at the end of this book for videos in which I demonstrate how to activate your grid.

Once more, after stating your affirmation, take a step back. See your intentions taking form in your mind's eye and fully believe it to be true. Feel the feelings; use all your senses and emotions to take in all the details of what it will be like when your goal translates into reality. Injecting strong senses, feelings and emotions into your visualizations empowers them with energy. The energy imprints the information (your intention) and programs it. We can liken this to programming a computer microchip. Energy is also used to imprint information onto a microchip (which is often made of quartz because of its programmability). This program then gets transmitted to source via your crystal grid. So, remember to be clear and focused yet calm with your intent so the message is sent "loud and clear". After a few minutes of this, simply release and let source energy take care of the rest. Don't dwell on it. You've set the wheels in motion and the crystal grid will continue to communicate your intentions. "The Force" is on the job now. The hard part is done.

The hard part may be done, but I don't condone forgetting about your grid all together. You don't need to do this entire activation exercise every time you happen to glance over at your grid. However, if your grid does get disturbed (those pesky kitties!), you will want to reactivate your grid exactly as described above. If nothing or no one ever disturbs your grid, do go ahead and reactivate it monthly...just to freshen up the intention and give it a nice energy boost.

Although we don't need to reactivate the grid all the time, you do want to give your grid some TLC and attention perhaps once a week, more often if you like. You can do this by meditating in front of the grid or simply directing your attention to it wherever you are, even if it's on the other side to the world. Remember the morphic field? *Tap into it!* You may want to do some energy work with your grid, such as Reiki. You can also simply sit and admire its beauty sending positive thought forms and powerful energy to your grid. Just don't ignore it.

Many ask me how long a grid should remain standing. I leave this totally up to you. If you feel the grid has completed its task you may take it down and do something else or you may want to leave it erected forever. Perhaps your grid will have worked its magic (oops! I mean "unknown science") in one day. I have had a grid set up for as short as one hour and taken it down because I knew its work was done. On the other hand, I have had some grids set up for some time and don't know if I will ever take them down. These include my healing grid and another I have set up for love and compassion. Do whatever you are called to do. Personally, I would not take a grid down if it has not accomplished its goal *unless* I realized there was a component missing or I have determined a way to redo it and make it better.

CHARGING OBJECTS IN A GRID

Do you have any items that can benefit from the energy of this grid or can combine their energies with it, enhancing it? It's a two way street, you know. For instance, perhaps you're going to do a crystal grid to assist you in getting a job. You can place objects within the grid that represent accomplishments you've achieved (a diploma or certificate). You may want to use some herbs and or essential oils that are known to enhance job-getting mojo. This can give your grid energy a powerful boost. On the other hand, you may want to boost the energy of objects that you can take away with you by placing them within the grid for a period of time to charge up. For example, you can place a piece of jewelry or a tie you will be wearing on your job interviews within your grid.

You can even charge yourself by creating a large crystal grid around you and sitting and meditating in the center of it. Some call this a crystal body layout. Alternatively, you could do a body layout on someone else and surround it with a clear crystal quartz outer grid creating profound amplification of the intentions. Just imagine the intensely potent energetic atmosphere if you meditated and visualized in the center of such a grid!

STEP BY STEP

Feel free to work with the energies and do what feels right and best for you. Always honor your own most powerful intuition. Having said that, many of my students appreciate being given some organized steps to follow until they feel confident enough to change things up on their own. So here's a checklist and some steps to get all your crystal grid components organized before you begin:

COMPONENT CHECKLIST:

- ❖ Center stone
- ❖ Surrounding stones
- ❖ Physical location, compass?
- ❖ Activation wand
- ❖ Photos, maps or names?
- ❖ Items to be charged?
- ❖ Outer grid?

PLANNING:

1. What is your intention?
2. What is your specific affirmation? (write it down)
3. What sacred geometric pattern will you use? Will you need to print out or draw a template?
4. Where will you physically locate your grid?
5. Use your compass to determine magnetic North, if you've chosen to do that
6. Will it require an outer grid?

THE STEPS:

1. Gather all your components including all necessary crystals
2. Create your sacred space
3. Go into an alpha state of mind and make your intention clear in your mind's eye
4. Set up your grid
5. Insert any objects you may be charging
6. Activate your grid while stating and feeling the intentions of your affirmation
7. Energize your affirmation with powerful visualization
8. Don't forget to pay attention to your grid. Take care of it with love, showing it some TLC ☺

CRYSTAL GRID HOW TO

In this section, I would like to take you through my thought process when I created a recent crystal grid.

A few months ago I decided to get absolutely clear with my future goals for my sacred crystal business. I spent some time meditating and journaling about exactly what that meant to me and what it looked like. Once I was very clear on what I desired and where I wanted the energies to go to achieve my goals I knew I needed to push my dream through with powerful energy. I knew with every cell in my being that my sacred crystal biz was my one true path and I was incredibly focused now on creating prosperity and abundance with my business so I could do it full-time. I know from past experience that just doing visualizations wasn't going to cut it and although I try to keep the negative mind chatter and thought patterns at bay; I'm not always perfect with it. Especially when those around you tend to drag you back into old habits. So, of course...*CRYSTAL GRID to the rescue!*

First, I jotted down notes on some post-it notes of appropriate crystals. I went through my collection specifically looking for crystals aligned to career and business mojo along with prosperity in a concentrated powerful punch. As I rummaged around my private crystal stockpile I came up with orange calcite, citrine, peridot, pyrite and lots of clear crystal quartz for amplifying. I also gathered up several green cloths and green candles. *Why all the green?* We associate the color green with growth, prosperity and abundance so that would provide an added layer of coordinated energy vibes. I laid all my chosen items out in front of me, trying different designs and making notes, sensing intuitively what felt best.

I finally narrowed it down to my large quartz point, "Big Baby" in the center surrounded by tumbled stones of orange calcite and citrine, intuitively knowing they were the right ones for the job. I used a lovely green peridot specimen in rock matrix at the base of the center stone and amplified the energy of the whole grid with small quartz lasers radiating outward from the whole design. I also decided to go with the green cloth flower of life grid template. As soon as I did that, I stood back and I knew it was right. *KA-POW!!*

*(Previous page) I laid out all my items and jotted down
notes as I thought everything through. That clear quartz
point is my hefty "Big Baby" at 8" tall.*

I mindfully put everything into place, carefully
following the flower of life design. I then also added
a few photos printed out from the Internet of things
and scenarios that reminded me of what life will be
like when my sacred business is in full swing and my
goal has been achieved. These were photos that
instantly made my soul sing! Weeeeeee!

For those of you that are wondering, YES, this crystal
grid is indeed *working its "unknown science!"* My
business is growing exponentially with total ease,
vitality and joy. These are all things that I set an
exceptionally strong intention for and set into
powerful motion with my crystal grid. Source energy
is now pushing it along.

My final stone selection: Big Baby as the center stone with a fine peridot specimen at its base surrounded by citrine, orange calcite and clear quartz lasers.

Practical Grid Recipes

Here are some practical crystal grid "recipes" you can start out with. Once again, feel free to tweak and experiment as much as you like. I am just giving a few ways to set up your grid here, but there are very many variables to experiment with and make your own. I highly encourage you to create your own grids, use the **Notes** section in the back of this book or the **Crystal Grid Worksheet** (you can also check the "Resources" section to find out where to print out multiples of a larger Crystal Grids Worksheet) and put your own energy into planning out a grid. *It will be so empowering for you.* As I like to say, "I present, you decide."

The crystals I have chosen for each grid have compatible crystal systems or "families" in order to enhance their energetic communications and thus make a more powerful grid. Keep in mind that clear quartz crystal is a great amplifier and can be used in conjunction or as a substitute to any stone with any of these grids or, again, as a supplementary outer grid to magnify the energies.

Relationship Enhancer: (of any sort of relationship): circle grid design, rose quartz (love and compassion), rhodochrosite (compassion, emotional healing) and blue lace agate (good communication); all belong to the hexagonal crystal system.

Attract or Enhance Romantic Love: hexagonal grid design, pink sapphire (love, open to romance), almandine garnet (remove fear, supportive, attract love relations) and ruby (passion, enthusiasm, self love); all contain aluminum. NOTE: You should never do this grid to attract any one *particular* person. You are simply attracting romance into your life, not trying to affect anyone's free will. Remember, worry about yourself and only yourself and never attempt to control anyone else. You can only control yourself.

Abundance and Prosperity: leminscate grid design, citrine (happiness, confidence booster, manifestation and creativity), green aventurine (vitality and growth) and green jade (abundance and joy); all are silicates. You may want to place some money under your center stone (if money is the type of prosperity you are trying to attract), or a bowl of fruit and bread to bring about plenty. You can get very creative!

Good Health: Flower of Life grid design, ruby zoisite (boosts life force and healing energy), green aventurine (good health and vitality) and amethyst (purification and elimination of toxins), all are silicates. If this grid is to help another individual, remember to get their permission first and then place under the center stone a photo of them when they were healthy.

Calm and Serenity: 5-pointed star grid design, amethyst (purification, protection and balance), rose quartz (stress relief, gentleness and calm) and lepidolite (relaxation, stress relief, calm); all are silicates. Candles with a calming scent such as lavender will really lend a nice boost to this grid.

Neutralizing Negativity/Self Protection: square grid design, 5 large black tourmaline pieces (neutralize and purify energy). Grid each outer corner of your home or a room, place 5th one in center. If gridding a home, the tourmaline may be buried underground (except for the center one which may be placed on display or in a safe natural container). If the home or room does not conform to a square shape, then try a triangle or 5-pointed star. Burning sage when working with this grid provides a good energy boost because sage attracts negative ions in an environment that is usually bathed in an overabundance of positive ions from electronics and such. This, in turn creates a positive experience for us. Please see the "Resources" section at the end of this book for information on negative ions.

Honoring Mother Earth: Phi spiral grid design, chrysocolla (feminine energies, connected to Earth energies), lepidolite (calming, supportive, connected with water element), larimar (feminine energies, ocean connection, tuned to Earth energies); all are silicates. They are also earth-healing stones which can counteract geopathic stress. When doing grids for Mother Earth or Peace on Earth I like to print out a large photo of the earth and place that under my stones.

Find a Job: hexagon grid design, carnelian (accept change and take action), ametrine (overcome fear of change, overcome procrastination), peridot (increases personal prosperity), citrine (manifesting and focusing your direction); all are silicates. You may include a picture of someone working in the career you are seeking, or a tool you may use while working at that new job.

Connection to Spirit: Flower of Life grid design,

apophyllite (connection to spiritual guides), ajoite (angelic connection and communications), amegreen (surrender to spirit, helps to awaken higher chakras); all are silicates.

Self Love Boost: leminscate grid design, rhodochrosite (healing of inner child, self acceptance), champagne tourmaline (acceptance of self and gentle self love) and eudialyte (love for self and emotional healing); all are of the hexagonal crystal system. Rose petals and essential oil are always nice to have around a love grid of any kind.

Happiness and Joy Infusion: circle grid design, carnelian (enhances joy of being alive, strengthens life force), tourmaline quartz (cleanses and purifies energy field), rainforest jasper (invigorates energy bringing renewal and pure joy); all are quartz. To infuse even more joy, a vase of live flowers would be perfect inside this grid.

Anxiety Banisher: 5-pointed star grid design, pink tourmaline (calming, soothes the heart), blue chalcedony (centers and balances emotions, soothes anxiety), lepidolite (balances and calms emotions); all are silicates. Remember to keep your affirmation positive; do not mention the anxiety. You may say something such as, "I am serene and tranquil, healing myself and moving through life's experiences with calm, grace, and ease".

You can take crystal grid creation in so many different directions and continue to build upon what you've learned here in this book. Of course, you are free to discard anything I've presented that doesn't quite ring true for you. There is no right or wrong way and the methods I've offered here are certainly not the only way. What I provide you with here are tools and guidelines. Again, I present the information, you decide. I hope this book has given you many ideas for you to work from and I dream that it's inspired you to continue to explore and to experiment on your own while you deepen your experiences and understanding of crystal grids. Astounding results can be achieved with crystals and stones so use this information in the most positive and healing way.

HAPPY CRYSTAL GRIDDING!

RESOURCES

The Book of Stones: Who They Are & What They Teach by Robert Simmons and Naisha Ahsian

The Crystal Healer: Crystal Prescriptions That Will Change Your Life Forever by Philip Permutt

International Center for Reiki Training: **http://www.reiki.org/GlobalHealing/Northandsout hpolehomepage.html**

Copper dowsing rods: **http://www.natures-energies.com/dowsing.htm** or **http://astore.amazon.com/hibiscusmoon-20/detail/B003115X5M**

My video on how to set up & activate a crystal grid: **http://youtu.be/BG2EFdrOEqw**

My video of me setting up for and activating a group Self Love crystal grid: **http://youtu.be/GHthKcqXBmA**

Check out **http://goldennumber.net** and **http://milan.milanovic.org/math/english/golden/gol den2.html** to read more and see many examples of Phi in nature.

Please see this site to read more about the Space Frame truss work design theory: **http://www.miqel.com/space_photos_maps/galactic _info/position-of-milky-way-in-virgo-supercluster.html**

WebMD explanation of how negative ions create positive vibes:
http://www.webmd.com/balance/features/negative-ions-create-positive-vibes

Visit **http://www.mindat.org** to find out about crystal systems and much more geological information on minerals.

Download 2 free crystal templates:
http://www.crystalgridsbook.com/crystal-grid-templates.html

References

Wikipedia, 2011:
http://en.wikipedia.org/wiki/Crop_circles

Ito, Hori, 1986:
Nobuoki, H. and Ito, S., 1966, *Electrical Characteristics of Triturus Egg Cells during Cleavage,*
http://jgp.rupress.org/content/49/5/1019.full.pdf

CRYSTAL GRID WORKSHEET

Use this worksheet to deepen your experiences and understanding of crystal grids and develop your skills in working with them. I suggest making several copies and keeping them together in a binder as a sort of journaling exercise that you can look back on and learn from your own practice and experiences.

Date: _____

What is the purpose and intention of this crystal grid?

List the all the components will you need:

Why did you choose the crystals you selected?

After creating your crystal grid and working with it for one week (or longer depending on the purpose of the grid), what were your experiences and results?

Do you think anything should be tweaked (if so, why?) or is this grid perfect as is?

Are there other crystals that you could try with this specific grid? If so, are these crystals that you should put on your "To Get" list?

Download PDF copies of this worksheet at
www.CrystalGridsBook.com

How About a FREE eKit to Help You Create Sacred Space Using Crystals?

Here's what's in this FREE Sparkly eKit:

- An MP3 download meditation. Relax and unwind with this 17:30 min. meditation. Let it guide you while you use a favorite crystal to help create a sacred space all of your own. Listen or download on your MP3 player. Downloading it allows you to keep it saved wherever you like to listen to again and again.

- A GORGEOUS photo-rich 57 page eBook filled with photos and stories of crystals & sacred spaces belonging to other sparkly souls such as yourself! Artists, Crystalline Cohorts, light workers, healers, crystal aficionados and spiritual hearts of all kinds have collaborated to come up with this *magical feast*.

- A 10 min. private video just for those who download this kit showing you how I personally use crystals in my sacred space...*a mini tour*!

- Plus you'll be signed up to my weekly emails always chock-full of crystal *YUMMINESS!*

Come along with all the other crystal hotties; stop by my website to subscribe:

http://www.hibiscusmooncrystals.com

LEARN ABOUT CRYSTAL HEALING ONLINE!

BECOME A CERTIFIED CRYSTAL HEALER

If you'd like to learn more about crystal grids from a video class and become a Certified Crystal Healer take a look at the Hibiscus Moon Crystal Academy!

Are you drawn to working with the energies of crystals and stones and feel you have a special connection with them? Would you like to enhance that connection? Would you like to use Mother Earth's gifts as an energy healing tool and support? You may even like to help others realize these powerful healing benefits by becoming a Certified and Accredited Crystal Healer. The Hibiscus Moon Crystal Academy has developed a curriculum and certification program like no other. This is not your run-of-the-mill crystal healer program. This course brings together physics and metaphysics to explain why and how crystals work. We'll explore all the newest research and use the science behind crystal vibration to develop you into a different kind of Crystal Healer!

www.HibiscusMoonCrystalAcademy.com

WOULD YOU LIKE TO MINGLE AND CHAT WITH OTHER CRYSTAL LOVERS?

Stop by and "Like" my Facebook page:
www.facebook.com/CrystalAcademy

We're always talking crystals and how to use them. Drop in and learn the science and fun behind crystal healing.

MORE CRYSTAL GRID STUFF!

Visit **www.CrystalGridsBook.com** for a free crystal grid template pdf download, photos of gorgeous crystal grids, sign up for Hibiscus Moon's email newsletter and more!

Visit Hibiscus Moon Crystal Academy website and blog at: **www.HibiscusMoonCrystals.com**

Like her on Facebook at:
www.facebook.com/crystalacademy

Follow her on Twitter at:
www.twitter.com/hibiscusmoon1

Visit Hibiscus Moon's YouTube Channel all about crystals at:
www.youtube.com/phanie12

ACKNOWLEDGMENTS

I would like to acknowledge and deeply thank the following people for their motivation, support and inspiration on this book-writing journey.

To my husband Frank, for his undying support, genuine excitement and faithfully making and bringing me coffee (with a straw) each day as I wrote. "Hand over fist!"

To my best friend, Cathy, for always supporting me in anything that I do, including our crystal circles at her house, always the ultimate hostess!

To my Crystalline Cohort students for your constant inspiration and dedication. I have learned so, so much from you and your experiences with crystal healing through your beautiful, wonderful and inspiring stories. I look forward to learning so much more.

To my Etsy customers, YouTube subscribers, blog readers, Facebook and Twitter friends for initially encouraging me to write a book, giving me advice and rooting me on to "get 'er done". Also, thank you for all the friendships and support from the very beginning.

To friend, teacher and mentor, M. Flora Peterson, for your never ending advice, super-support, knowledge and talents.

To friend, mentor and guide, Melanie Wallace, for

teaching me so much and for all your advice and encouragement.

Lastly, but certainly not least, many thanks to you, dear reader, for reading this book. You're a GEM! ;)

ABOUT THE AUTHOR

Hibiscus Moon has learned to channel her inner geek then merge it with her serious obsession with crystals and stones, bringing her unique perspective to the world of crystal healing. As a National Board Certified Professional Science teacher, Hibiscus Moon delivers the science behind the metaphysical aspects of working with crystals. As a Certified Crystal Master and Registered Metaphysician, Hibiscus Moon speaks, teaches and writes about crystals and is the founder and director of The Hibiscus Moon Crystal Academy where she certifies others to become Certified Crystal Healers. She resides in Florida with her husband and kitty, Topaz, aka "Topaz Panina Meow Meow".

NOTES

NOTES

NOTES

NOTES

NOTES

NOTES

NOTES